# The Miracles of Jesus

## The Insight Series

### Ken Schauers

CONCORDIA PUBLISHING HOUSE • SAINT LOUIS

Written by Ken Schauers

Edited by Robert C. Baker

Scripture quotations are from The Holy Bible, English Standard Version®. Copyright © 2001 by Crossway Bibles, a publishing ministry of Good News Publishers, Wheaton, Illinois. Used by permission. All rights reserved.

Hymn texts with the abbreviation *LSB* are from *Lutheran Service Book*, copyright © 2006 by Concordia Publishing House. All rights reserved.

This publication may be available in braille, in large print, or on cassette tape for the visually impaired. Please allow 8 to 12 weeks for delivery. Write to Lutheran Blind Mission, 7550 Watson Rd., St. Louis, MO 63119-4409; call toll-free 1-888-215-2455; or visit the Web site: www.blindmission.org.

Manufactured in the United States of America

1 2 3 4 5 6 7 8 9 10                    16 15 14 13 12 11 10 09 08 07

# Contents

---

**Hymnal Key**

*LSB = Lutheran Service Book*
*ELH = Evangelical Lutheran Hymnary*
*CW = Christian Worship*
*LW = Lutheran Worship*
*LBW = Lutheran Book of Worship*
*TLH = The Lutheran Hymnal*

# About This Series

This course is one of the Insight Series of short (four-session) adult Bible study courses, each looking at an important biblical topic or theme. Using these courses, you will gain insight into a portion of the Scriptures as you hear what God is saying to you there about Himself, about yourself, and about His Good News of salvation in Jesus Christ. These insights will help you as you go about your disciple's task of living in the Word, and will equip you for a more fruitful study of the Word on your own in the future.

## Using This Course

This course is designed to be used for small-group discussions. Each of the four 60- to 90-minute sessions you will find in this booklet will provide you with a clear picture of where the session is going and what it is supposed to accomplish, give you a way to lead into the session's study, provide input and discussion questions to guide your study of the text, suggest ways to follow up on the study during the week, and offer closing worship aids.

You will not need a teacher for this course. The printed material will guide you through the study. No one will have to be the answerer. But you will get the most from these materials if you:

1. Assign a leader for each session. That person should:

   a. Make sure he or she works through the material before the session and, if possible, looks at some additional resources to enrich your study.

   b. Begin and end the session with worship. The devotional time may be quite brief; a prayer or a Bible reading is sufficient. You might assign the opening and closing to a worship leader for each session.

   c. Keep the discussion moving. There is a tendency to get

bogged down on some questions or points. The leader should be willing to say, "We'd better move on to the next point."

d. Make some choices if time is limited. The leader will want to select those items from the session's content that seem to be most helpful if it is clear there will not be time to work through all of the material.

e. Listen. Make sure everyone is heard. Give each a chance to speak. Encourage participation.

f. Pray for all participants.

2. Prepare for each session. The discussion will work better, the material will be more meaningful, and the Word will speak more clearly if everyone in the class works through the session's material before the class session. Even if preparation is limited to reading through the texts that will be a part of the session's study, the effort will enrich your study.

3. Meet regularly (at least once a week) in a convenient and comfortable place. Too much time between sessions means that learning will be forgotten and much time will be used in constant review. Too little time between sessions does not allow time for you to connect what you have learned to your daily living.

4. Provide resources. Preparation that includes a chance to look at commentaries, Bible dictionaries, Bible reference books, maps, and so on will add to your class. Encourage those who do such research to contribute what they have learned or discovered as you study.

5. Encourage participation. The course offers many opportunities to discuss biblical texts and to talk about application of the Word to each individual's life. The key is sharing. Everyone should have a chance to listen and to be heard. The goal is encouragement. We want to build one another up as we study the Word. We want to share the hope and the strength we receive by the power of the Spirit through that Word. We want to allow each person to come closer to the Savior as he or she encounters Him in the Word. Emphasize the positive. Share the joy of the Gospel. Celebrate His promised presence as "two or three" gather in His name.

# Participant Introduction

*The Miracles of Jesus* will help you look closely at several of Jesus' miracles so that you can see more clearly how His miracles revealed His identity and His mission. In so doing, you will be able to reaffirm what those miracles say to you about the activity of our Savior in our lives today. This study will give insight not only into the miracles under study, but also into all Jesus' miracles. You will discover what those miracles meant to the people who first experienced them and what they mean for us.

Ken Schauers

## ∝ Session 1 ∾

# Jesus Touches Lives through Miracles

## Our Goals for This Session

By the power of the Spirit working through the Word, we will

* see Jesus revealing Himself to us through His miracles;

* understand what His miracles are telling us about ourselves and about His relationship to us.

## Getting Started

Read John 4:46–54 and Mark 2:1–12. Put yourself in the crowds that witnessed these events in Jesus' life. Imagine that these two events were the only contacts you have had with Jesus. What would be your impression of Him? On a separate sheet of paper answer the following questions.

Suppose you were going to describe Him to someone else—someone back in your village. All you know about Him is what you have experienced in these two healing miracles. What would you say about Him?

Share your description aloud with the class or in small groups. How are your descriptions alike? How do they differ?

What impressions of Jesus are common? To what extent were you able to see Him in these passages as Savior?

# Into the Word

## Seeing Jesus as God and Man

1a. React to this statement: "While Jesus was on earth, He was a true man. He had the same feelings, needs, concerns as any man. He was tempted, put under stress, frightened, angered, frustrated, as all of us are. He did not pretend to be human. All of what it means to be a human being (except sin) was true of Him." Do you agree?

*Jesus was true God & true man. Jesus was in man but he had no sin.*

b. Why is it sometimes difficult for us to see Jesus as a real human being?

c. Why do we tend to emphasize Jesus' divinity over His humanity?

*Takes both God & man for our Salvation.*

*Jesus Raises A Widow's Son*

Though Jesus was human, He often revealed His divinity as He dealt with people. Read these Bible accounts: Luke 5:12–15; 7:11–17; Matthew 9:1–7; John 6:1–15. Page through the Gospels and read and summarize some of the other miracles of Jesus.

*Jesus feeds the Five Thousand*

*Jesus Walks on Water meets the needs of the people*

2a. Which of these seem to be most important? Why?

*Turning water into wine.*

*Healing Based on faith)*

*no limits what Jesus can do.*
*Compassion).*

b. In each case, what did the miracle say about Jesus? List what each tells us about Him.

c. What was the reaction of the people who observed Jesus' miracles? Why did they react that way?

d. How did Jesus' miracles point to the truth that He is both human and divine? What would the miracles have meant to you?

*Would make you a believer .*

## Reasons

3. Jesus occasionally gave reasons for His miracles. What reasons do you find in the following passages?

a. Matthew 9:6

*Forgiveness to forgive sin.*
*Power of Jesus miracles*

b. John 9:1–5

*Work of God*

*All for the Glory of God. Jesus brings light into the world.*

4. What do you think those reasons have to do with all of Jesus' miracles?

# Reading the Miracles as Law and Gospel

On one hand, Jesus' miracles are Law. They remind us of our own weaknesses and frailties.

5. How do you see that message in the following passages?

a. Matthew 17:14–21

*disciples faith not strong enough to cast out the questions.*

b. Mark 11:12–23

*faith.*

6a. How do miracles speak Law to you?

*faith is the key to miracles that speak law*

b. What effect does the accusation of the miracle have on your life?

*We are to grow & mature in our faith.*

On the other hand, Jesus' miracles are Gospel. They tell us that Jesus has power over sin and the powers of evil, and solutions to our problems and needs.

7. How does Jesus show His power in the following passages?

a. Matthew 8:28–34

*Jesus drives out demons by His power*

b. Luke 10:17–20

c. Matthew 12:22–28

8. How do we see Him as the solution to the problem of our sins in the following passages?

a. Mark 2:1–11

b. Luke 23:34, 42–43

9a. How do these and other miracles of Jesus give you comfort and assurance?

*The Lord demostates more than what we can comprehend. but its reassuring to me that God is with us.*

b. What do the miracles mean to you?

*God is in charge.
Be Thankful for what we have.*

## The Greatest Miracle

Jesus' greatest miracle was His bodily resurrection from the dead. Read Matthew 28:1–10 (and parallels).

10a. What were the reactions of those who witnessed the resurrection? *Keepers did shake & became as dead men. Fear came upon them They were afraid.
There was also great Joy.*

b. How do those reactions compare to the reactions to Jesus' other miracles?

*They departed with great joy & fear*

11. What does the resurrection of Jesus say to us about Him? (See Romans 1:4.)

*Now to him that worketh is the reward not reckoned of grace, but of debt.*

12a. How did the miracle of the resurrection affect Thomas (John 20:24–29)? *Because Thomas had seen him, Thou hast believed.*

b. What blessing does Jesus have for Thomas? for us?

*To be faithful and believe*

Read 1 Corinthians 15:1–28.

13a. What is the importance of the miracle of Jesus' resurrection? *The resurrection of Jesus is all important. It is the all.*

b. What does Jesus' resurrection mean for you?

*Victory over death*

c. What guarantee is there for you?

*The truth of God's Word. and His Promise.*

13

d. Why is the resurrection the most important miracle in knowing who Jesus is and what He has done?

*Jesus paid for our sins. We can come to the Father without any sin.*

14a. How would you describe the miracle of the resurrection to someone else? What hope and joy do you find?

b. How can you share that hope and joy?

*Share the Good News.*
*Live the faith.*
*Share has been given to me.*
*Love — Sharing —*

## His Miracles Continue

Jesus' miracles show us what we were designed to be.

15. In what way do the following passages show us our potential?

a. Luke 10:17–20

*Rejoice — We are citizens of Heaven*

b. Mark 16:17–20

*Go & preach everywhere*
*Jesus was taken up into heaven and sat on the right hand of God*

c. Matthew 21:18–22

*The power of Prayer has no limit.*

d. John 14:12–14

*Power in Jesus name and asking in Jesus name & Pray.*

e. Acts 3:1–10

*What I give to you I give in the name of Jesus Christ.*

16. What do the texts mean for you?

17. In what sense are His miracles still working through you? Talk about it.

# In Conclusion

A sharing exercise: Ask for volunteers to share a time when God worked in their lives in a miraculous way.

18a. Talk about the good that happened from the miracles. How was God present?

b. How was He revealing Himself?

c. What part did Jesus and His promises have in the miracles? *The impossible became possible.*

d. What did the miracles accomplish?
*Going to further the kingdom of God.*

19a. What danger might there be in "looking for" a miracle?

b. Where are we to find our greatest assurance of the love, protection, and salvation of Jesus?

c. Why can what we think to be miracles sometimes lead us astray?

## To Do This Week

ભ Read through as much of the Gospels as you can. Note each miracle of Jesus.
• What is special about each?

• What is each saying to you about Jesus? about yourself?

• What questions remain?

ભ Share your notes, insights, and questions with the class next time you meet.

## In Closing

Close with a prayer in which volunteers may add a petition or word of thanks, or read the following prayer.

Prayer: Lord of the universe, our heavenly Father, we thank You that You make Your mercy known through Your miracles. We praise You that You show us Your love in Christ through His miracles. Make us receptive to Your Word and the power of Your Holy Spirit. In Jesus' name. Amen.

Close by singing or reading in unison "O Sons and Daughters of the King" (*LSB* 471:1–4, 9; *ELH* 366; *CW* 165; *LW* 130; *LBW* 139; *TLH* 208).

> Alleluia, alleluia, alleluia!
>
> O sons and daughters of the King,
> Whom heav'nly hosts in glory sing,
> Today the grave has lost its sting!
> Alleluia!
>
> That Easter morn, at break of day,
> The faithful women went their way
> To seek the tomb where Jesus lay.
> Alleluia!
>
> An angel clad in white they see,
> Who sits and speaks unto the three,
> "Your Lord will go to Galilee."
> Alleluia!
>
> That night the apostles met in fear;
> Among them came their master dear
> And said, "My peace be with you here."
> Alleluia!
>
> On this most holy day of days
> Be laud and jubilee and praise:
> To God your hearts and voices raise.
> Alleluia!

# ଔ Session 2 ଖ

# Jesus Touches Lives by a Multiplication of Resources

## Our Goals for This Session

By the power of the Spirit working through the Word, we will

- understand what God is revealing to us about Jesus in Mark 6:30–44; *Feeding the 5000 5 loaves bread 2 fish*
- evaluate the impact of that miracle on our lives;
- move toward action as we support the ministry of Christ today.

## Getting Started

Ask someone to read Mark 6:30–44 aloud. As you listen, close your eyes and pretend you are sitting on the grass three rows from Jesus. Try to imagine a lonely place, a great throng, a compassionate Jesus, anxious disciples, five loaves of bread, two fish, and twelve woven baskets. Now open your eyes. What do you imagine the crowd was thinking as Jesus spoke to the disciples? as the disciples handed out the bread and fish? as their stomachs became full and their appetites were satisfied? Share your thoughts with the group.

# Into the Word

## A Look at Mark 6:30–44

Read verses 30–31. These verses indicate that the disciples were under some stress. (The word *apostles* in the text is probably used to distinguish them from the disciples of John mentioned in v. 29.)

20a. Describe their stress. Was it a spiritual or temporal concern? Was it selfishness or a concern for others?

*Temporal Concerns —*
*Disciples concerned for themselves*

b. How does their cause for stress compare to yours?

c. How do you react when you are under stress? *Pray*
*Eat – rest*

Read verses 32–33.

21. Why might the arrival of the crowd have been somewhat stressful for Jesus?

22. Why had He gone across the lake?

*to find a solitary place & get some rest. To have a place to mediatate*

23. How might you have responded in this situation?

24. What does Jesus' reaction say about Him?

Read verse 34. Seeing the crowds, Jesus was moved to compassion. He satisfied the people's spiritual needs by teaching them.

25. Contrast Jesus' attitude to the attitude of the disciples. How do you account for the difference?

*Disciples consumed with temporal concern*
*Jesus concern about the spiritual side*

26a. Which attitude, compassion or disinterest, do you find most common among Christians today? Why?

*People our selfish.*

b. How about in your life? Which attitude do you find most often?

*Temporal is overriding the spiritual*
*Mixed, I have temporal concerns which override the spiritual.*

Read verses 35–37. These verses zero in on the attitude of the disciples.

27. See if you can write a brief description of some possible reasons for their attitude. Which of the following seem(s) possible to you? Give reasons for your choice(s).

21

a. The disciples were frustrated.

*They need rest & food. The crowd followed them & the disciples worked hard for the people.*

b. The disciples were tired.

*Self interest instead of being mineful of others.*

c. The disciples did not want to use what would have amounted to about nine months' wages for the cause.

28. Which of the preceding reasons sound most familiar to you? Why are they all easy to use?

*Human nature.*

29. Describe a time when you felt like the disciples. What happened?

30. What changed your attitude? If you were able to overcome the feelings that interfered with your ability to serve, what helped you?

Read verse 38. The lunch provided is five small loaves of bread and two (probably dried) fish.

31a. What do you suppose the disciples said to themselves as Jesus handed them these few scraps to pass out?



b. What might have been your reaction?



Stop 32. The number seven (five plus two) might have significance in itself (such as the six days of Creation plus the Sabbath), but it is especially important as a contrast to the number twelve (the baskets left) and the number five thousand. What do the numbers say to you about Jesus? about His miracle?



Read verses 39–42. After meeting the crowd's spiritual need (verse 34), Jesus feeds the people.

33. The promise that God will feed His people and the fulfilling of that promise is often repeated in the Old Testament (see Exodus 16:1–5; 1 Kings 17:1–6; Deuteronomy 8). What might the people have thought as they saw Jesus doing what God had promised?

34a. Compare the Mark passage to John 6:5–15. How does the fact that Jesus fulfilled Old Testament promises explain the reaction of the people in verses 14–15?


b. What did they see in Him?


# The Miracle for Us


In this miracle Jesus took the resources that the disciples had at their disposal and multiplied them to meet the needs of people. This same Jesus is with us today. He has the same power now as He did then to multiply the resources that you have.

35. Make lists like the following of your available resources:

| Time | Talents and Skills | Treasures |
|------|--------------------|-----------|
| 1–2 p.m. Thursday | Able to knit<br>Able to teach<br>Have knack for . . . electronics | Garden<br>Savings account |

36. Make another list of services you can perform, such as taking the elderly shopping.

Put a cross by the gifts and actions you are now giving to the Lord so that He can multiply your resources.

37. What other resources might you give to the Lord for multiplying?

# In Conclusion

38. Write a brief description of the truths about Jesus you learned from the study of this miracle. What is God revealing to you about the Savior in this account?

39. Write something you learned about yourself from the study of this miracle. What may God be trying to help you see more clearly?

40. Share how you were brought more fully to the realization that you are in constant need of the love and forgiveness of God in Jesus by the study of this text.

41. Share something you have decided to do in response to the love of God in Jesus because of your study of this miracle.

## To Do This Week

ცჳ Bake or buy some bread and share it with someone who is hungry. Then share the Good News of God's love in Jesus with someone who is hungry to hear it.

• How does God bless each sharing?

• What other ways can you share with those in need?

ცჳ Tell about your sharing experiences with your class members at your next session.

## In Closing

Close with a prayer (spoken or silent) asking God to multiply your resources so that they may be a blessing to others. Ask for volunteers to add a petition asking God to supply special gifts and graces as the members of the class go about the task of sharing the Good News.

Close by singing or reading in unison "Lord of Glory, You Have Bought Us" (*LSB* 851; *ELH* 459; *CW* 486; *LW* 402; *LBW* 424; *TLH* 442).

Lord of glory, You have bought us
    With Your lifeblood as the price,
Never grudging for the lost ones
    That tremendous sacrifice;
And with that have freely given
    Blessings countless as the sand
To the unthankful and the evil
    With Your own unsparing hand.

Grant us hearts, dear Lord, to give You
    Gladly, freely of Your own.
With the sunshine of Your goodness
    Melt our thankless hearts of stone
Till our cold and selfish natures,
    Warmed by You, at length believe
That more happy and more blessed
    'Tis to give than to receive.

Wondrous honor You have given
    To our humblest charity
In Your own mysterious sentence,
    "You have done it all to Me."
Can it be, O gracious Master,
    That You deign for alms to sue,
Saying by Your poor and needy,
    "Give as I have giv'n to you"?

Lord of glory, You have bought us
    With Your lifeblood as the price,
Never grudging for the lost ones
    That tremendous sacrifice.
Give us faith to trust You boldly,
    Hope, to stay our souls on You;
But, oh, best of all Your graces,
    With Your love our love renew.

# Jesus Touches Lives through Faith

## Our Goals for This Session

By the power of the Spirit working through the Word, we will

* see how Jesus works through the faith of His people;

* evaluate the impact of His work on our lives;

* receive God's grace in His Word and Sacraments so that our own faith is strengthened.

## Getting Started

Take a moment to think of the person you know who has the "greatest" faith. Without using names, write a description of that person and his or her faith on a separate sheet of paper. What makes faith evident in that person's life? What does faith do for him or her? What kind of a resource is faith for his or her daily living? What word most clearly describes the person you are thinking of?

Meet in small groups and share your descriptions. Talk about them. What is common in each description? What is unique? What characteristics of faith-filled people can you list? How are those characteristics present in you?

# Into the Word

## Two Miracles

Read Matthew 15:21–28 and Matthew 8:5–13 aloud.

42. What similarities and differences do you see? List some of them.

43a. In each case Jesus commends the person's faith (see 15:28 and 8:10). What was notable about the faith in each case?

b. What was the most important characteristic of that person's faith?

44a. What did the fact that each was a Gentile have to do with his or her faith?

b. How does that fact make their faith even more remarkable?

45a. Jesus calls their faith great, yet these were not "great" people—at least not by the world's standards. What does the fact that the greatest faith belonged to ordinary people—those who might not even have been expected to *have* faith—say to you?

b. What does that say about faith today?

c. What does it say about your faith?

# Responding to a Need

Read Matthew 15:22.
46a. What was the Canaanite woman's need?

b. How pressing was the need? how unselfish?

47a. When have you experienced such a need? What did you do?

b. How did you seek help? What did Jesus have to do with the response to that need?

Read Matthew 15:23.

48. What was Jesus' response to the woman's outcry of need?

49. Imagine for a moment what the woman felt like after she asked the Savior of the world for help, and He was silent. Share some of the feelings she may have experienced.

50. Talk about some of the times when you asked God for help, and He was silent. How did you feel? What did you do?

51. Reflect on a time when Jesus cried out to God and God seemed to be silent (see Matthew 27:45–46). Even though God

was silent at that point, how do we know that He was working for the good of everyone?

52a. When we call for help and God is silent, what may the silence mean?

b. What should we do when God seems to be silent?

c. How can we be encouraged, even when God does not seem to answer? Share some of your insights.

53a. What is the disciples' response to this woman in need?

b. What does their attitude say about our response to the needs of others?

c. How can we see in Jesus a way to become more sensitive to others' needs?

# Great Faith

Read Matthew 15:24, 26, 28.

54. Why do you think Jesus appeared to reject the woman? What might He have been trying to teach her? to teach His disciples?

55a. In spite of silence and rejection by the disciples and Jesus, what was the woman's response (v. 25)? What might we have expected of the woman?

*Lord help me — Go away g home*

b. What might have been your reaction?

*I don't know*

c. How might you react today if someone (pastor, friend) who was supposed to help you rejected you?

Read Matthew 15:27. This verse displays two elements of a great faith: (1) the woman agreed with Jesus that she did not deserve His grace; with the word "yes" she admits she has a right to demand nothing; (2) and with the words "Yet even the dogs eat the crumbs that fall from the master's table," she throws herself on the mercy of her Lord; she trusted in His promise of love, mercy, and forgiveness.

56. Compare her response with our Confession and Absolution as we speak and hear it on Sunday morning. What do we deserve? What do we claim? On what do we depend?

*We deserve his temporal & eternal punishment — Claim his mercy. We depend on his resurrection*

57. The woman's faith did not cause Jesus to respond. What caused His response? *Grace*

58. The woman's faith received His response of love. How does our faith receive the gifts He has for us? Why must we always understand faith as God's gift and not our work (see Ephesians 2:8–9)?

*By Grace you have been saved.*

59a. What promises of God (e.g., Romans 8:28) are most important to you? Why?

b. How do those texts speak to you when you are troubled or in need? How can you share them with others?

*God therefore us. He's not going to leave us —*

60a. In what sense is your faith "great"?

b. What great gift does it receive?

c. How does the constant love and forgiveness that God has for us in Jesus help us receive His great gifts, even when our faith does not seem great?

# In Conclusion

61. Write a brief description of the truths about Jesus you learned from the study of these miracles. What is God revealing to you about the Savior in these accounts?

*Jesus is truly the Son of God. Jesus is with us always*

62. Write something you learned about yourself from the study of these miracles. What may God be trying to help you see more clearly?

63. Share how studying these texts brought you more fully to the realization that you are in constant need of the love and forgiveness of God in Jesus.

64. Share something you have decided to do in response to the love of God in Jesus because of your study of these miracles.

## To Do This Week

ଓ Keep a "faith" diary. Each day, jot down the "great" things God has done for you and through you.
• What is He accomplishing in your life?

• Take note of the times when your faith seems less than

great. How does that realization bring you back to your Savior for strength and forgiveness?

• How do you seek to cling to His promises when faith falters?

ೞ Share some of your experiences with your fellow class members at your next session.

# In Closing

Close with a prayer (spoken or silent) asking God for a great faith, or read this prayer:

Prayer: Merciful God, we confess to You that at times our faith is weak. We often doubt, turn to our own way, ignore Your commands and promises. Call us back by the power of Your Spirit through Your Word. Help us to trust more fully in Jesus who bought eternal life for us. Teach us to come to Him with every need and to cling to Him in every trial. We thank You for the gift of our faith. Open our hearts to the work of the Holy Spirit, who gives us this precious gift through Your Word. In Jesus' name. Amen.

Close by singing or reading in unison "To Thee, Omniscient Lord of All" (*LSB* 613; *LW* 234; *LBW* 310; *TLH* 318).

> To Thee, omniscient Lord of all,
> In grief and shame I humbly call;
>> I see my sins against Thee, Lord,
>> The sins of thought and deed and word.
> They press me sore; I cry to Thee:
> O God, be merciful to me!

O Lord, my God, to Thee I pray:
O cast me not in wrath away!
    Let Thy good Spirit ne'er depart,
    But let Him draw to Thee my heart
That truly penitent I be:
O God, be merciful to me!

O Jesus, let Thy precious blood
Be to my soul a cleansing flood.
    Turn not, O Lord, Thy guest away,
    But grant that justified I may
Go to my house at peace with Thee:
O God, be merciful to me!

# Ꮆ Session 4 ᎷᎷ

# Jesus Touches Lives with His Word

## Our Goals for This Session

By the power of the Spirit working through the Word, we will

- realize that Jesus our Lord has all things under His control;

- learn to turn to Him when we find ourselves in troubled waters;

- seek the strength and power of His Word to overcome our troubles and problems.

## Getting Started

Ask a volunteer to read Matthew 14:22–33 aloud. As you listen, close your eyes and pretend you are in the second seat of that boat with the disciples. Imagine the strong wind, the darkness, the hungry waves.

Our text says that the disciples were terrified. What thoughts do you think went through their minds? Were they concerned only about themselves, or perhaps also their families?

Share your answers with someone else. Have you or they experienced similar situations? What did you feel at the time? What role did Jesus play in your experience?

# Into the Word

## Water Can Mean Trouble

Read Matthew 14:22–24. The water in this account, as in many places, is a conveyor of evil. Look up and discuss some of the following:

65a. What did Jonah believe happened to him when he was thrown into the water in Jonah 2:3–4?

b. What did the water mean for him?

66. What is the psalmist's attitude toward the waters in Psalm 69:1–2?

67. What impression is given about the waters in Psalm 77:16–18?

68. What evil comes out of the sea in Daniel 7:3 and Revelation 13:1? (Check a commentary for an interpretation of those images.)

69. What did water do in Genesis 7 and Exodus 14?

70. What will the water do in the end times? (See Luke 21:25–26.)

71. Summarize the attitude toward water given by these passages.

72. What reason can you find here that might account for the reluctance of many at Jesus' time to travel by boat?

73a. The disciples were not just plagued by a bad storm, but they were also plagued by the evil represented by the waters that seemed out to get them. When have you had a similar experience?

b. When has something beyond your power seemed determined to hurt or destroy you? Describe your experience.

c. What was the result?


74a. What light does Ephesians 6:10–12 shed on the power of evil to destroy us or do us damage?


b. If the goal of evil is to "sink the Christian," how does this Word of God respond?


c. What does that assurance mean for you?

*Victory over Satan.*


## From Fear to Hope

Read Matthew 14:25–27.

75. At first the disciples were terrified. Why? Why might they have thought that Jesus was a ghost?

76. Compare their experience here with John 20:19–21. Check the context. How was their fear similar? How different?

77a. Jesus appears and deals with their fear in the same way both times. What does He say?

*Peace be with you.*
*Don't be afraid.*

b. What are His words meant to do for the disciples?

*Calm them down*
*Eliminate there fear.*

78. Look at the "fear nots" in the following passages. How do they speak to your fears? How do they assure you of Jesus' presence? How do they help? Think about and discuss each passage.

a. Genesis 26:24

*I am your God of Father of Abraham. Do not be afraid for I am with you. Reassurance of Him being with me.*

b. Isaiah 41:10

*Do not fear I am with you I am your God.*

c. Isaiah 43:1–2

d. Matthew 10:30–31

# A Venture of Faith

Read Matthew 14:28–29.

79a. Peter could have asked Jesus to make the storm go away. What does he ask instead? Why?

b. What might have been his reason for seeking that favor?

80a. What was the result?

b. Why do you think Peter failed? What was the cause of his faltering faith? *Peter took his eyes off Jesus. and began to doubt.*

81. When have doubts and/or a misdirected faith caused

you to "sink"? Share an event like that. What hope or help did
you find? How did help come to you?

82a. What help for sinking times do you find in Psalm
50:15; Romans 8:28, 31–39; and similar passages?

*Call upon me in the days of
trouble & will deliver you, & you
will honor me*

b. How can you share that hope with others who are sinking?

*stop* ¹⁰/₁₉

# His Helping Hand

Read Matthew 14:30–31.
Compare John 21:15–17. Remember the context and how
Peter had denied Jesus at the courtyard of the high priest.
83. In what way was Jesus keeping Peter from sinking in
both of these events?

*Jesus knew Peters heart. Jesus
knows all things & all our heart*

84. What is the significance of the fact that Jesus "reached
out" to Peter during both of these events?

*If we ask we will receive Jesus
does take care of us .*

85a. If Peter had told you about both of these happenings, what might he have said?

b. What would he have said about Jesus? about himself?

*God is always faithful in our lives & he truly loves us. We all need Jesus' help.*

c. What do you think Peter learned?

*We all need Jesus help.*

86a. What does Jesus reaching out to a doubting, sometimes-denying Peter tell us about Him?

*Jesus doesn't give up on us. His Grace is sufficient. God's riches at Christ expense.*

b. What assurance can we gain from this look at Jesus? What help for troubled times? Share that assurance and hope with one another.

*Complete Assurance. His Love is always there. We have Blessed Assurance. Ours is the final victory over sin & death.*

## In Conclusion

87. Write a brief description of the truths about Jesus you learned from the study of this miracle recorded in God's Word.

*Jesus is our helping hand.*

46

What may God be revealing to you about the Savior in this account?

88. Write something you learned about yourself from the study of this miracle. What may God be trying to help you see more clearly? *We all need Jesus help.*

89. Share how studying these texts brought you more fully to the realization that you are in constant need of the love and forgiveness of God in Jesus.

90. Share something you have decided to do in response to the love of God in Jesus because of your study of this miracle.

# In Closing

Conclude with a prayer (spoken or silent), asking God for confidence in His strength when we face evil or troubles. Or read one of the Psalms that speak of our confidence in God's love for us in the midst of troubles, such as Psalm 23, 55, 121. Or ask each person to select and share his or her favorite passage of comfort.

Close by singing or reading in unison "Eternal Father, Strong to Save" (*LSB* 717; *LBW* 467).

Eternal Father, strong to save,
Whose arm hath bound the restless wave,
Who bidd'st the mighty ocean deep
Its own appointed limits keep:
O hear us when we cry to Thee
For those in peril on the sea.

O Christ, whose voice the waters heard
And hushed their raging at Thy word,
Who walkedst on the foaming deep
And calm amid its rage didst sleep:
O hear us when we cry to Thee
For those in peril on the sea.

Most Holy Spirit, who didst brood
Upon the chaos dark and rude,
And bid its angry tumult cease,
And give, for wild confusion, peace:
O hear us when we cry to Thee
For those in peril on the sea.

O Trinity of love and pow'r,
Our people shield in danger's hour;
From rock and tempest, fire and foe,
Protect them wheresoe'er they go;
Thus evermore shall rise to Thee
Glad praise from air and land and sea.